NASA astronauts, may I be your plus-one? —S. M.

For Kenny & Charlotte, my faraway friends —S. L.

For future astronauts (or Marsonauts, as I like to call them) —M.

Henry Holt and Company, *Publishers since 1866*
Henry Holt® is a registered trademark of Macmillan Publishing Group, LLC
120 Broadway, New York, NY 10271 • mackids.com

Library of Congress Control Number: 2020910085
ISBN 978-1-250-25688-1
Our books may be purchased in bulk for promotional, educational, or business use. Please contact your local bookseller or the Macmillan Corporate and Premium Sales
Department at (800) 221-7945 ext. 5442 or by email at MacmillanSpecialMarkets@macmillan.com.
First edition—2021 / Design by Cindy De La Cruz
The artist used colored pencils and digital tools to create the illustrations for this book.
Printed in China by RR Donnelley Asia Printing Solutions Ltd., Dongguan City, Guangdong Province

7 9 10 8 6

OUR UNIVERSE

MARS!
EARTHLINGS WELCOME

BY MaRS (WITH STACY McANULTY)

ILLUSTRATED BY MaRS (AND STEVIE LEWIS)

Henry Holt and Company ✳ New York

You're Invited!

MISSION TO MARS

WHEN: AS SOON AS POSSIBLE
(BUT PROBABLY NOT FOR A FEW DECADES)

WHERE: ON MARS (OF COURSE)

Hello, inhabitants of Earth—or, as she calls herself,

Planet Awesome.

You're Invited!

MISSION TO MARS

WHEN: AS SOON AS POSSIBLE
(BUT PROBABLY NOT FOR A FEW DECADES)

WHERE: ON MARS (OF COURSE)

I'm formally inviting you to visit me!

Planet Marvelous!

Let me introduce myself.
I am Magnificent Mars.
Favorite sibling of Earth.

Fourth planet from Sun.

Second smallest in the solar system.

You've spent so much time on Earth—
probably your whole life. It's time you visited me.

Some people have been to Earth's Moon,
but no one has ever been to another planet.

MOVE TO MARS

And I'm a planet. A party planet!
I want to be the FIRST planet with human guests.

How to Be a Planet
(in our solar system):

Orbit Sun.

Be round.

Don't be a "dwarf planet."
Sorry, Pluto.

How to Be a Party Planet:

Invite friends.

Be classy, not gassy.

MARS

MARS

MARS

TO: VENUS

URY

TO:
NEPTUNE

TER

Jupiter

Neptune

Saturn

Uranus

I'm close to you.
Sorta. Depending
on my orbit.

Earth and me at our closest,
34 million miles apart.

But sometimes, siblings need space,
and we're 250 million miles apart.

You'll love it here.

I'm like Earth—kinda—only better.

For example, my day is longer. Thirty-seven minutes longer.

Earth.
One spin.
24 hours.

Me!

One spin.

24 hours AND
37 MINUTES!

Think of what you can do with 37 extra minutes!

Sleep in. Enjoy more screen time. Eat junk food.

Whatever you want.

And I have two moons!
I know Earth is totally jealous.

Say hi to Phobos and Deimos.

You might mistake them for ginormous potatoes.
Nope, they're natural satellites.

When you come, bring a camera. There's so much to see.

Guess who has the
largest volcano in the whole
SoLaR system?

Not Earth.
Me!

OLYMPUS MONS

Olympus Mons is 16 miles tall. Earth's biggest active volcano, Hawaii's Mauna Loa, is not even half that height.

MAUNA LOA

Do you like stunning views?

Valles Marineris is four times as deep as the Grand Canyon!

And not nearly as crowded. Great place for a selfie.

Along with your camera, don't forget to BYOO!

That means "bring your own oxygen." Because, well, I don't have much. Just a trace.

Pack water, too, because all of mine is frozen.

Scientists think I had liquid water millions (maybe billions) of years ago, when I was warmer.

Lakes.

Rivers.

Oceans.

Today, I'll admit, Earth totally wins
when it comes to liquid H_2O!
She's a better planet for swimming.

Yep, Earth is blue and known for her water.
Especially her Ocean.
I'm red, not because I'm hot.
My average temperature is −81°F.
Colder than the South Pole in winter.

I'm red, not
because I'm mad.
But that's probably why Earthlings
named me after the Roman god of war.
War. Blood. Anger. You get it.

I'm red because my soil
is full of iron—rusty iron.

Earth and I, we're rocky, rugged planets.
Mercury and Venus, too.

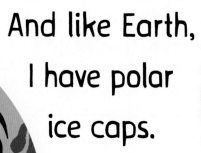

(Jupiter, Saturn, Uranus, and
Neptune are gas giants!)

And like Earth,
I have polar
ice caps.

I have mountains.
I have clouds.

And I have dreams!

Dreams of big-brained visitors who want to travel to Miraculous Mars.

If you think parties on Earth are fun, **just you wait!**

But this invitation isn't for my birthday.

I don't know my *exact* birthday. I'm about 4.5 billion years old, like all the planets in our solar system.

I've had "visitors" from Earth in the past,
but none with a heartbeat.
In 1965:

The US spacecraft *Mariner 4*, my first flyby.
It came within 6,118 miles and took 22 pictures.
I hope it got my good side.

In 1971: *Mars 3*, a Soviet craft, actually landed on my surface and operated for a whole 20 seconds.

In 2004,
NASA sent me new friends—
Spirit and *Opportunity*.

These cute rovers were expected
to play and explore for only 90
days. But I'm so impressive, they
scampered around way longer.

Spirit.
Six years.

Opportunity.
Almost 15 years!
This little guy traveled 28 miles.
(That's longer than a marathon.)

Still, I long for you humans with your curious minds, your five senses, and your love of parties.

Imagine the things we'll learn.

Imagine the fun we'll have.

So what are you waiting for?
Come to reMARkable Mars!

Let's get this party started!

As soon as your spaceship* is ready.

*new technology required

Dear Potential Mars Visitors,

Earthlings have yet to set foot on Mars, but it's on our to-do list. NASA currently has a long-term goal of sending astronauts to explore the red planet, though this will be decades in the making.

What steps must we take before that can happen? First, we need to know whether there has ever been life on Mars. Second, we need more information about the climate. Third, we have to continue exploring the geography. Ultimately—and hopefully—this will take us to the final phase: human visitors.

Our first human-to-Mars trip is certain to be long, dangerous, and amazing. So, who wants to go?

Sincerely,

Stacy McAnulty

Author and wannabe Martian astronaut

P.S. Every day, scientists are learning more and more about our solar system. (Yay, science!) So some details may change as our knowledge expands. But hey, that's to be expected, right?

Mars or Earth or Both?

Who can claim the following statements?

1. "Two is better than one, especially when it comes to moons."

Mars. He has two oblong moons: Phobos and Deimos. Phobos, the larger satellite, is gradually moving closer to Mars. Smaller Deimos is moving farther away. (Earth and her one Moon are BFFs.)

2. "My ice caps are totally cool. Get it? Cool."

Both. Mars has ice caps at both his North and South Poles. Earth also has ice caps (though they are smaller than those of Mars), and she has giant ice sheets in Antarctica and Greenland. These ice sheets hold 99% of Earth's freshwater supply.

3. "Maybe my magnetic personality is because of my magnetic field."

Earth. A compass on Earth will point toward the "magnetic north pole." Earth's magnetic field isn't just good for directions; it also helps keep the planet safe from solar radiation. Mars does not have a magnetic field now, but evidence shows he had one in his past.

4. "Canals are human-made rivers, and I've got 'em."

Earth. Earth's famous canals include the Suez, Erie, Grand, and Panama. In 1906, Percival Lowell wrote a book titled *Mars and Its Canals*, in which he claimed that the planet had Martian-made waterways. He considered this evidence of ancient life on Mars. Percival was wrong.

5. "I'm a named pet of a Roman god."

Mars. Mars was the Roman god of war. Phobos is Greek for "fear," and deimos is Greek for "terror." War, fear, terror—quite a scary trio of names. Earth is just named for Earth.

6. "We're not big balls of gas; we're both a lot more rocky."

Both. Mars and Earth are terrestrial (or rocky) planets. They have a core, a mantle, a crust, and some form of atmosphere. Mercury and

MARS by the Numbers

Mars is the fourth planet from Sun.

142,000,000 — The average distance between Sun and Mars is 142 million miles. (To compare, Sun and Earth are 93 million miles apart.)

1,477 — A Martian day (one rotation on his axis) is 1,477 minutes, or 24 hours and 37 minutes.

687 — A Martian year is approximately 687 Earth days long.

4,220 — Mars's diameter is 4,220 miles, which is a little over half of Earth's diameter.

34,000,000 — The closest Earth and Mars get is 34 million miles apart.

250,000,000 — Earth and Mars can be 250 million miles apart when on opposite sides of the solar system.

A Brief History of Humans and Mars

Since Mars is visible with the naked eye, it does not have a date of discovery or a discoverer.

1610 — Galileo observed Mars through a telescope.

1877 — Asaph Hall discovered Mars's moons.

July 14, 1965 — The US spacecraft *Mariner 4* took the first up-close picture of Mars.

December 2, 1971 — The Soviet probe *Mars 3* made the first soft landing on Mars and operated for 20 seconds.

January–March 1989 — The Soviet craft *Phobos 2* orbited Mars and Phobos, transmitting information for several days before malfunctioning.

July 4, 1997 — NASA's Mars *Pathfinder* landed and deployed *Sojourn*, the first wheeled rover, which explored for 83 days.

January 3, 2004 — NASA's rover *Spirit* landed on Mars, and three weeks later *Opportunity* touched down on the opposite side of the planet. Both rovers were designed for 90-day missions, but *Spirit* operated until March 2010 and *Opportunity* until June 2018.

2020 and beyond — NASA's Mars Exploration Program (MEP) is a multistep mission to learn more about Mars and ultimately prepare for human exploration.

Sources

Encyclopaedia Britannica "Percival Lowell: American Astronomer." Accessed March 9, 2020. britannica.com/biography/Percival-Lowell.

Encyclopaedia Britannica "Planet." March 13, 2020. britannica.com/science/planet.

Howell, Elizabeth. "A Brief History of Mars Missions." Space.com. April 8, 2019. space.com/13558-historic-mars-missions.html.

Malin, Michael C., Michael J. S. Belton, and Michael H. Carr. "Mars." In *Encyclopaedia Britannica*. March 13, 2020. britannica.com/place/Mars-planet.

NASA Science. "Mars Exploration Rovers." Mars Exploration Program. Accessed Sept. 10, 2019. mars.nasa.gov/mars-exploration/missions/mars-exploration-rovers/.

NASA Science. "Mariner 3 & 4." Mars Exploration Program. Accessed Sept. 10, 2019. mars.nasa.gov/mars-exploration/missions/mariner-3-4/.

NASA Science. "Mars Facts." Mars Exploration Program. Accessed Sept. 10, 2019. mars.nasa.gov/all-about-mars/facts/.

NASA Science. "Mars: The Red Planet." Solar System Exploration. Accessed June 14, 2019. solarsystem.nasa.gov/planets/mars/overview/.

National Snow and Ice Data Center. "Quick Facts on Ice Sheets." Accessed Sept. 10, 2019. nsidc.org/cryosphere/quickfacts/icesheets.html.

Nine Planets. "Mars Facts." March 6, 2020. nineplanets.org/mars.html.

Redd, Nola Taylor. "Mars' Moons: Facts About Phobos & Deimos." Space.com. Dec. 8, 2017. space.com/20413-phobos-deimos-mars-moons.html.